CIRCULAR
IN THE
DERBYSHIRE
DALES

by
JOHN N. MERRILL
(Footslogger)

Maps and photographs by John N. Merrill.

a J.N.M. PUBLICATION

1992

1

a J.N.M. PUBLICATION,

**J.N.M. PUBLICATIONS,
WINSTER,
MATLOCK,
DERBYSHIRE.
DE4 2DQ**
☎ **Winster (0629) 650454**
FAX **Winster (0629) 650416**

Edited, typeset, designed, paged, marketed and distributed by John N. Merrill.

© Text and routes - John N. Merrill   1992.

© Maps and photographs - John N. Merrill   1992.

First Published -   January 1992

ISBN 0 907496 99 7

Meticulous research has been undertaken to ensure that this publication is highly accurate at the time of going to press. The publishers, however, cannot be held responsible for alterations, errors or omissions, but they would welcome notification of such for future editions.

Typeset in - Eagle book and bold and Bookman - bold, italic and plain 9pt and 18pt.

Printed by - John N. Merrill at Milne House, Speedwell Mill, Miller's Green, Wirksworth, Derbyshire. DE4 4BL

Cover sketch by John Creber - "River Wye Bridge, Bakewell - © J.N.M. PUBLICATIONS 1992.

An all British product.

CONTENTS

Hi!
- a few notes
about
Footslogger.

He was born in the flatlands around Luton in Bedfordshire, but his athletic capabilities soon showed themselves on Sports Day and in the football and cricket teams. Although expelled twice from different schools, he moved to Sheffield and was taken out into the Peak District at the age of 6 1/2. Here he ran up and down the rocks and the sense of enjoyment and freedom has never left him. He was hooked on the outdoors for life. By the age of 15 he had 350 books on the Himalayas and other mountain areas and although failed all eight O levels, he was writing a book on the history of mountaineering! At 16 he soloed the 90 foot high school building and the headmaster rushed him off to Outward Bound Mountain School to be properly trained - he thought it was a fantastic holiday!

At 17 he was chosen with eleven others to go on an expedition to Norway, for a month. Since then he has walked more than 150,000 miles in different parts of the world. He has walked The Cleveland Way 8 times; The Peakland Way 14 times; The Limey Way 14 times; The Pennine Way 4 times; Offa's Dyke 3 times; Pembrokeshire Coast Path 3 times; and all the other official paths at least twice.

He is an avid walker and never known to be really tired; likes to carry heavy loads at 18,000 feet and hates having his socks or shirts washed after a six month walk! His ideal day is a 25 mile walk with three bars of chocolate in his pocket. Having worn out nearly fifty pairs of boots he truly lives upto his nickname, Footslogger!

INTRODUCTION

The Derbyshire Dales area of the Peak District contain some of the finest limestone dale walking in England. For many years I have wandered down them from all angles and never tiring of seeing their stunning beauty whatever the season. Here in this book are ten of my favourite walks in the area - two are in the gritstone country around Eyam and Baslow, but they only enhance the variety of walking found.

The walks take in many dales with the popular and majestic Monsal Dale with a high and low level route. Chee Dale is rugged and hard and is an exceptional walk. Lathkill Dale will always remain a "special" dale for it is so picturesque and full of unique variety. Lesser known dales of Bradford, Gratton and Long Dale are explored together with the limestone area around Parwich and Hassop. One short walk explores the old lead mining village of Winster.

Here then are some exciting walks among the limestone dales, except one, there is at least one inn along the way! May the sun shine all day as you explore these dales seeing the rich variety of scenery, wild life and flowers.
Happy walking!

John N. Merrill

John N. Merrill
Winster.

ABOUT THE WALKS

Whilst every care is taken detailing and describing the walk in this book, it should be borne in mind that the countryside changes by the seasons and the work of man. I have described the walk to the best of my ability, detailing what I have found on the walk in the way of stiles and signs. Obviously with the passage of time stiles become broken or replaced by a ladder stile or even a small gate. Signs too have a habit of being broken or pushed over. All the route follow rights of way and only on rare occasions will you have to overcome obstacles in its path, such as a barbed wire fence or electric fence. On rare occasions rights of way are rerouted and these ammendments are included in the next edition.

The seasons bring occasional problems whilst out walking which should also be borne in mind. In the height of summer paths become overgrown and you will have to fight your way through in a few places. In low lying areas the fields are often full of crops, and although the pathline goes straight across it may be more practical to walk round the field edge to get to the next stile or gate. In summer the ground is generally dry but in autumn and winter, especially because of our climate, the surface can be decidedly wet and slippery; sometimes even gluttonous mud!

These comments are part of countryside walking which help to make your walk more interesting or briefly frustrating. Standing in a farmyard up to your ankles in mud might not be funny at the time but upon reflection was one of the highlights of the walk!

The mileage for each walk is based on three calculations -

1. pedometer reading.
2. the route map measured on the map.
3. the time I took for the walk.

I believe the figure stated for each walk to be very accurate but we all walk differently and not always in a straight line! The time allowed for each walk is on the generous side and does not include pub stops etc. The figure is based on the fact that on average a person walks 2 1/2 miles an hours but less in hilly terrain.

EQUIPMENT NOTES
.... some personal thoughts

BOOTS - *preferably with a full leather upper, of medium weight, with a vibram sole. I always add a foam cushioned insole to help cushion the base of my feet.*

SOCKS - *I generally wear two thick pairs as this helps minimise blisters. The inner pair are of loop stitch variety and approximately 80% wool. The outer are a thick rib pair of approximately 80% wool.*

WATERPROOFS - *for general walking I wear a T shirt or cotton shirt with a cotton wind jacket on top. You generate heat as you walk and I prefer to layer my clothes to avoid getting too hot. Depending on the season will dictate how many layers you wear. In soft rain I just use my wind jacket for I know it quickly dries out. In heavy or consistant rain I slip on a neoprene lined gagoule, and although hot and clammy it does keep me reasonably dry. Only in extreme conditions will I don overtrousers, much preferring to get wet and feel comfortable. I never wear gaiters!*

FOOD - *as I walk I carry bars of chocolate, for they provide instant energy and are light to carry. In winter a flask of hot coffee is welcome. I never carry water and find no hardship from not doing so, but this is a personal matter! From experience I find the more I drink the more I want and sweat. You should always carry some extra food such as Kendal Mint Cake, for emergencies.*

RUCKSACKS - *for day walking I use a climbing rucksack of about 40 litre capacity and although it leaves excess space it does mean that the sac is well padded, with an internal frame and padded shoulder straps. Inside apart from the basics for one day I carry gloves, balaclava, spare pullover and a pair of socks.*

MAP & COMPASS - *when I am walking I always have the relevant map - preferably 1:25,000 scale - open in my hand. This enables me to constantly check that I am walking the right way. In case of bad weather I carry a compass, which once mastered gives you complete confidence in thick cloud or mist.*

EYAM MOOR & WARDLOW - 12 MILES

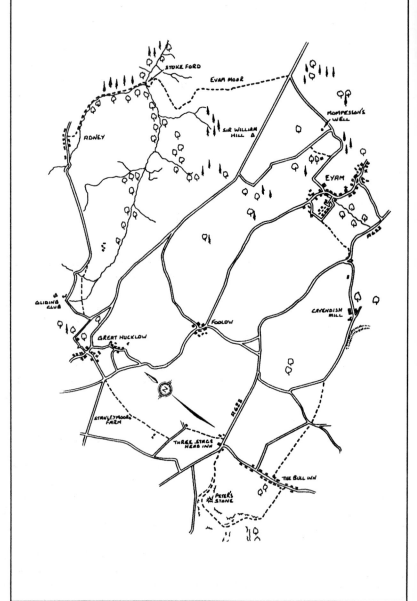

EYAM MOOR & WARDLOW - 12 MILES
- allow 4 to 5 hours.

⚑ - *Eyam Car Park—Eyam YHA—Mompesson's Well —Eyam Moor—Stoke Ford—Abney Clough— Abney—Great Hucklow—Stanleymoor Farm— Stanley House—Wardlow Mires— Peter's Stone —Wardlow—Cavendish Mill—Middleton Dale — Eyam.*

🚗- *Eyam on Hawkhill Road. Grid Ref. SK216768.*

 - O.S. 1:25,000 Outdoor Leisure Map—The White Peak - East sheet.

🍺 - *Several in Eyam; one in Great Hucklow; Three Stag's Head, Wardlow Mires; Bull's Head Inn, Wardlow.*

ABOUT THE WALK - Starting from Eyam the walk takes you into the gritstone country across moorland and clough before descending to the limestone plateau and through one of the loveliest dales of the Peak District. To regain Eyam you cross the Stoney Middleton area renowned for its limestone quarries and rock faces. There are three 'pubs' en route and either Great Hucklow or Wardlow Mires makes a good lunchtime halt.

WALKING INSTRUCTIONS - From the car park turn right and ascend the single track road, bearing right at the bend at the top. A few yards past the entrance to Eyam Youth Hostel on your left, leave the road via the wooden stile. The path at first is ill-defined but after crossing the stile turn left before ascending beside the wall of the hostel grounds. Above the hostel stop and look behind you for the view down on to Eyam is quite exceptional. You are now on level ground and after crossing two fields you gain a minor road from Highcliffe. There is a right-of-way from the road past Ladywash Mine to Stoke Ford but nothing exists on the ground. Turn right at the road and follow it to the road junction 1/4 mile away. Turn left and head due north along a 'B' road towards Eyam Moor. A short distance along here you pass on your

Mompesson's Well where, during the plague which ravaged Eyam in 1666, William Mompesson the Rector of Eyam left money in vinegar water.

Half a mile later where the old road over Sir William Hill meets yours at a sharp right-hand bend, ascend the ladder stile and follow the footpath across Eyam Moor, keeping the wall on your immediate right. The wide path is signposted to Stoke Ford and Abney. The next couple of miles to Abney is some of the finest walking in the Peak district and I never tire of this section. First the path crosses heather-clad moorland before weaving its way down to Stoke Ford. Here you cross two bridges before following the signposted path to Abney via Abney Clough. For the first part of the walk you go through woodland then into grass fields. Abney is reached via a farm track. Turn left in the village and walk along the minor road towards the gliding club. About 3/4 mile along here, at the farm track to Abney Grange, use the wooden stile and cross the field. Cross three fields to a shuttered building, 400 yards south of the entrance to the gliding club. The stone stile is on the left of the building and a gentle ascent from here across two fields brings you to a minor road. Turn left and, where the road turns left a short distance later, turn right and follow a track through the trees and down to Great Hucklow village.

On gaining the main street in the village turn left then right, almost due south as you walk out of the village to a cross roads. Opposite is the footpath sign and track to Stanleymoor Farm. Follow this for 1/4 mile to the farm where you turn left and cross five fields to a tarmac lane, 1/4 mile away, just south of Stanley Lodge. Turn left along the lane to the entrance of Stanley House. At the house entrance turn right and cross the field diagonally, heading almost southwards. Two further fields bring you to the eastern side of Wardlow Mires. Turn right beside the A623 road, passing the Three Stags Head inn on your right. Just past the road junction (B6465) to Wardlow on your left, walk in front of a small cottage on your left to a stile and the start of the footpath through the northern end of Cressbrook Dale.

This particular section is one of my favourite limestone walks. The path hugs the valley floor and skirts round the base of the prominent limestone outcrop—Peter's Stone. A 1/4 mile later and just past the entrance to Tansley Dale, you begin ascending the left-hand side of the dale to its rim. The view from the top is more than reward for your labour. At the top you walk due east following a walled footpath to Wardlow, 1/3 mile away. At the road (B6465) turn left into the village passing The Bull inn on your right. A few yards later you pass a chapel on your right and immediately after is the stile and path towards Cavendish Mill. The actual path line is faint but all the stiles are there. You are basically heading due east for 2/3 mile. The final section to a minor road is through a lead mining area. At the minor road go straight across and use the stile opposite. The right-of-way from here should now go diagonally leftwards, but has been fenced off. Instead you keep straight ahead beside the fence until you come to a wooden stile on your left near the top of the field. Here turn left to a stone stile in the field boundary opposite. From here you can pick up the true line of the right-of-way as you head north-easterly to a stone stile just over the brow of the field. Over this you head for the road you can now see. There should be a stile here but there isn't!

Turn right along the road and descend to Cavendish Mill. Quite a contrast to some of the beautiful scenery you have seen on the walk—especially on Eyam Moor. However, Stoney Middleton area has numerous quarries seeking its valuable limestone. It is one of the ironies of the Peak National Park that it not only is an exceptional scenic area but also extremely rich in minerals. Upon reaching the mill, turn left down the road between the buildings. In a very short time you are descending a single track lane through attractive scenery. At the bottom of this shallow dale you meet the A623 road. Cross over and a little to your right is the path to Eyam. At first it is a wide track as it skirts round the base of limestone faces. Then you begin ascending a well used footpath reaching the top of Middleton Dale via a series of steps with a hand rail! Now head almost due north as you ascend gently a field. Near the top go over a stone stile into the next field to reach a farm building and walled lane.

Walk along this and at the road junction, three fields later, keep straight ahead. Use the footpath a short distance ahead on your right, and descend between the houses to the main road through Eyam. Turn left and shortly afterwards right up Hawkhill Road to the car park where you began, perhaps five hours ago. Although one of the longest routes in the book, few walks in the Peak District have more variety—moorland, hamlets, limestone dales and industry.

BASLOW EDGE & CHATSWORTH PARK - 6 MILES

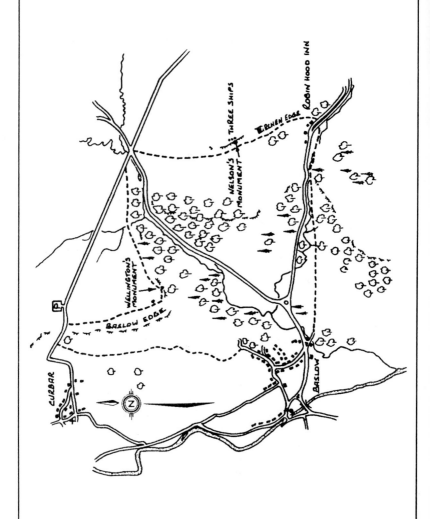

BASLOW EDGE & CHATSWORTH PARK - 6 MILES - allow 2 1/2 hours

- Curbar Gap—Baslow Edge—Wellington's Monument—Birchen Edge—Robin Hood Inn—Chatsworth Edge— Chatsworth Park — Baslow— Baslow Edge—Curbar Cap.

 - Curbar Cap. Grid Ref. SK263748.

 - 1:25,000 Outdoor Leisure Map—The White Peak - East sheet.

 - Robin Hood Inn, Birchens.

ABOUT THE WALK - The gritstone edges are one of the 'wonders of the Peak District' and deservedly so. Their bold lines on the rim of the escarpments provide excellent rock climbing routes and view points for the central area of the National Park. This short walk takes you to three edges at the southern end of the edge system and across open country. There is a 'pub' at the halfway point!

WALKING INSTRUCTIONS - From the car park at Curbar Gap, turn right and walk down the road a short distance before turning left up a grass track to a gate and ladder stile. From here you follow a wide track along the top of Baslow Edge, which you do not see but will walk beneath on your return. The views from Curbar Gap are quite exceptional down on to Curbar and the River Derwent. Northwards are the impressive rock faces of Curbar Edge. Walk along the track for 1/2 mile, walking almost due south to reach the Eagle Stone, often referred to as the 'Aigle Stone' and named after a giant called Aigle who could lift stones heavier than anyone else. It is also said that before you marry you must climb the stone !

Bear left and follow the path to Wellington's Monument, erected in memory of the Iron Duke who died in 1852. The view from here is also extensive, especially down to Chatsworth Park. Across the valley on the top of Birchen Edge can be seen the pillar of Nelson's Monument. Turn left at Wellington's Monument and follow the track for 3/4 mile to the road to Curbar Gap. Go through the small gate on the right and turn right to the road junction with the A621 road. Cross the road to the road opposite and the ladder stile is a few strides from the junction on your right. Over this and you are in open country. A path can be seen heading almost due south to Birchen Edge, and this you now follow.

Nelson's Monument on top of Birchen Edge was erected in 1810 by John Brightman of Baslow. Closeby to the 12 ft. pillar are three stones known as the Three Ships. They look a bit like the bows of a ship and have carved on them the names Victory, Defiant and Royal. Continue along the path at the base of Birchen Edge. At the end of the path ascend the ladder stile and turn right to the A619 road, passing the Robin Hood Inn on your right; you are now halfway ! At the road turn right and almost immediately left and follow the concessionary foot-path through Chatsworth Park to Baslow 1 1/2 miles away. First you descend some steps, crossing a bridge before following a wide track to your right and passing the gritstone buttresses of Chatsworth Edge on your left. At the end of the track there is a huge stile to ascend before entering the open country of Chatsworth Park. As you walk through the northern end of the park you head almost due east.

After passing a wood on your right you reach the main path into Chatsworth from Baslow. Turn right into Baslow, via a large metal kissing gate. As you enter Nether End (Baslow) you pass a thatched cottage on your right and cross a bridge over Bar Brook. There are shops, inns, cafes, toilets and car park here. Leave the Nether End section of Baslow via the road, Eaton Hill, on the immediate right of the Ye Olde Cottage Cafe. At the top of the road turn right and walk up the 'No Through Road'—Bar Road. As you ascend past the houses the road becomes a rough track. Just past the houses the track turns sharp right; here you turn left and follow the path beneath Baslow Edge. These gritstone edges are a marvellous rock climbing ground and are extremely popular during the weekends. As you walk past the edges you will no doubt see numerous people scaling easy and hard routes. For the first half of the section back to Curbar Gap, about 1/2 mile, you keep a stone wall on your left. Beyond is a 1/3 mile of open country before reaching a few stone walls and the road. Turn right up the road to the car park and the starting-out path. Again savour that view down to Curbar and beyond.

REMEMBER AND OBSERVE THE COUNTRY CODE

 Enjoy the countryside and respect its life and work.

 Guard against all risk of fire.

Fasten all gates.

 Keep your dogs under close control.

 Keep to public paths across farmland.

Use gates and stiles to cross fences, hedges and walls.

  Leave livestock, crops and machinery alone.

 Take your litter home - pack it in; pack it out.

 Help to keep all water clean.

 Protect wildlife, plants and trees.

 Take special care on country roads

Make no unnecessary noise.

MONSAL DALE
HIGH LEVEL ROUTE - 7 MILES

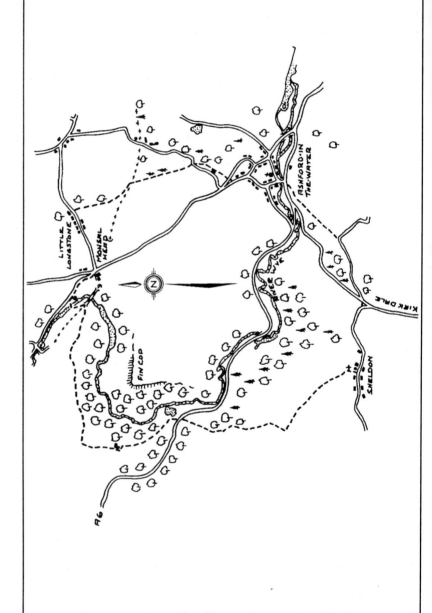

MONSAL DALE
- HIGH LEVEL ROUTE
- 7 MILES
- allow 2 1/2 hours.

◄● �„● ◄● *- Ashford-in-the-Water—Little Longstone—Monsal Head—River Wye—Brushfield Hough—A6—Sheldon—Kirk Dale—Ashford-in-the-Water.*

- Ashford-in-the-Water—off eastern end of Fennel Street, at Grid Reference SK 194698 (public convenience).

- 1;25,000 Outdoor Leisure Map—The White Peak - East sheet.

- Monsal Head Inn; Packhorse Inn, Litle Longstone; two in Ashford in the Water.

ABOUT THE WALK - Monsal Dale is the Queen of the Dales' in the Peak District. No other has such a stunning location and one never tires of gazing at its beauty. It is only natural that such a scenic wonder is one of the most popular places of the National Park. This walk takes you to Monsal Head to admire the view but instead of walking along the dale floor beside the River Wye, the route takes you high along the dale's rim. In doing so you have wonderful views all the time of the dale from different angles. The walk, keeping to its 'high level' theme, includes two limestone villages—Little Longstone and Sheldon. The final stage is a descent into Ashford-in-the-Water which is more than a fitting climax to one of my favourite walks in the Peak District.

WALKING INSTRUCTIONS - Leave the car park via the tarmac footpath on the left-hand side, along the edge of the football field. At the end of the path turn left up Hill Cross and at the road junction 200 yards later bear right. A further 200 yards later leave the road via the stile on your right and cross a small field to the B6465 road. Turn left then right almost immediately and follow the signposted footpath to 'Little Longstone 2 miles'. The mileage is wrong for when you reach Little Longstone the other sign says 1 1/2 miles! The path is well defined and well stiled. After 1/4 mile cross the minor road to Great

Longstone and continue walking across the field to the old Buxton-Matlock railway line. Cross this and turn left for a short distance before crossing three fields to the eastern side of Little Longstone village. Turn left and walk along the road through the village, passing the Pack Horse Inn on your right, to Monsal Head.

The view from Monsal Head is breathtaking. Walk along the road past the Monsal Head Inn and where the road turns sharp right and descends steeply towards Crossbrook, the limestone stile is opposite. Turn right down the path and descend to the farm at the bottom of the dale. Turn left at the end of the building and cross the River Wye via the footbridge. On the opposite side take the path which diagonally ascends to your left and begin your climb to the rim of Monsal Dale. After crossing the dismantled Buxton-Bakewell railway line, you continue ascending up a walled lane. After 300 yards the wall ends and you keep to the farm track as it swings away from the dale side for a short period. The next half mile is along this well defined track which provides delightful views down Monsal Dale and its railway viaduct. After 1/2 mile you go through two gates and after the second you turn left through a field gap and head for the track to the farm—Brushfield Hough. As you do so you have further views of the dale especially of Fin Cop. Walk through the farm to its southern end and turn left through the gates to the farm road. Follow this for 200 yards and where the road turns sharp right, on your left is the stile and path to the River Wye and A6 road. The Ordnance Survey map shows the right-of-way going straight down but the path on the ground zig-zags its way and you should follow this. Cross the wooden ladder stile over the stream and ascend to the A6 and car park opposite.

From the car park use the stile above parking spaces and follow the well trodden path around the hillside to the entrance to Dimin's Dale. Ascend the stile and cross the dale floor and keep straight ahead ascending between the limestone outcrops. After 300 yards, as signposted for Sheldon and Ashford, begin climbing the diagonal path to your left to the edge of Great Shacklow Wood. Upon reaching the stone wall and stile, don't go through but turn right and ascend steeply keeping the wall on your left to the stile at the top. Once there you have no more climbing to do! The path now heads due south for two fields and after the second stile you turn sharp right to a walled lane. Here turn left and follow an intermittent lane to Sheldon 1/2 mile away. The route is well stiled and in the final stages you have a walled lane to walk along. You reach Sheldon after passing the parish church, dedicated to St. Michael and All Angels, on your left, which is a useful landmark.

Gaining the road in Sheldon turn left and follow it for 1/3 mile and where it turns sharp right to descend to the road in Kirk Dale, turn left and use the stile and path to the road cutting out the large bend. At the road junction continue ahead on the minor road signposted for

Ashford. the road gently ascends along the edge of Arrock Plantation. After 1/3 mile where the road turns sharp right turn left through the small gate and begin descending the signposted path to Ashford in-the-Water. The path takes you past a radio mast before going gently down the fields and past a farm to the A6 road opposite the Sheepwash Bridge. As you descend you have magnificent. views on to Ashford and over the area you have walked- you can see Monsal Head and Little Longstone very clearly. Cross the road and enter Ashford via the historic Sheepwash Bridge. Continue straight ahead along Fennel Street and the car park is at the top on your right. Before leaving Ashford, and if time permits, the parish church with its Norman tympanum, examples of Ashford marble and funeral garlands is well worth exploring.

MONSAL DALE - 1 1/2 MILES - LOW LEVEL ROUTE

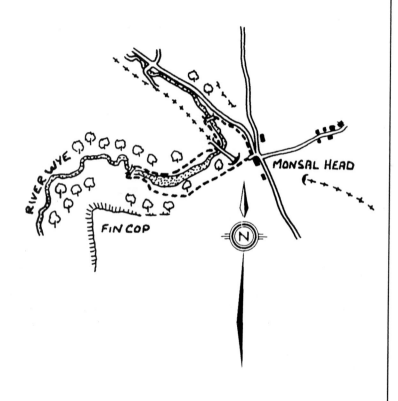

MONSAL DALE
(Low Level Route)
- 1 1/2 MILES
- allow 3/4 hour

- Monsal Head—River Wye—Monsal Dale Weir — Monsal Head.

 - Monsal Head. Grid Ref. SK 185715.

 - 1:25,000 Outdoor Leisure Map—The White Peak - East sheet

 - Monsal Head.

ABOUT THE WALK - The shortest walk in the book! I make no apologies for including this one for the walk makes a really pleasant stroll on a summer's evening.

WALKING INSTRUCTIONS - Start from the Monsal Head car park and walk along the road to the viewpoint down on to the viaduct, dale and weir. Continue to where the road turns sharp right and descends towards Cressbrook. Your path and stile are opposite. Go through the stile and turn right and descend to the dale floor and farm. At the opposite end of the building turn left and cross the River Wye via the footbridge, and follow the path that keeps to the dale floor near the river. After 300 yards you walk under the high railway viaduct and swing away from the river for a short distance, returning to the river at Monsal Dale weir.

The tumbling water is always an enthralling sight. On the river can be seen coots, moorhens and mallard ducks, and during the early summer many nest in the area. Continue down the right-hand side of the Wye to the footbridge. Here cross the river and begin your gradual climb through the trees back to Monsal Head a little over 1/2 mile away. As you ascend you have further views of the dale especially to Cressbrook. You reach Monsal Head and viewpoint via a stone stile. All you have to do now is to retrace your steps around the Monsal Head Inn to the car park, after savouring yet again that unsurpassed view of Monsal Dale.

CHEE DALE &
CHELMORTON - 9 MILES

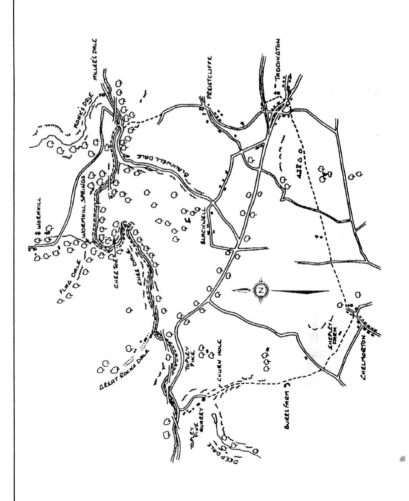

CHEE DALE & CHELMORTON - 9 MILES
- allow 3 to 4 hours

- *Topley Pike—Churn Hole—Burrs Farm—Shepley Farm—Chelmorton —Trig Point 438 Metres— Taddington—Priestcliffe—Miller's Dale—Chee Dale—Topley Pike.*

- *Beside A6 at the entrance to Chee Dale. Grid Ref: SK104725.*

- *1:25,000 Outdoor Leisure Map—The White Peak - East sheet.*

- *Church Inn, Chelmorton; Queen Anne Inn, Taddington.*

ABOUT THE WALK - In its 2 1/2 mile length, Chee Dale is unsurpassed in Derbyshire for its variety and grandeur. It has the tallest limestone buttress and one of the longest limestone faces in the county. To make upward progress through the dale you have bridges and stepping stones to use. This walk takes you through the entire length of the valley but first you cross the limestone plateau at its highest before reaching the dale.

WALKING INSTRUCTIONS - From the car park, head southwards to cross the A6 and walk up the road to Topley Pike quarry. On your left you will see a footpath sign—'Chelmorton'. Keep to the left-hand side at the top of the road and start following a footpath, which is fenced for a short distance. Just past the quarry buildings on your right, turn left and walk up Marl Dale - a short dale with limestone buttresses at the end. There is a path which zig-zags its way up them and as you ascend you pass two deep potholes. They are part of a small cave system known as Churn Hole. At the top of the rocks you ascend a stile and, still heading southwards, walk beside a wall on your left. Where the wall turns sharp left you keep straight ahead aiming for the left hand side of Burrs Farm. There are stone stiles all the way. Just past the farm you go over a stile and walk up a walled track to 'Old Coalpit Lane' (A5270).

Cross the road and as indicated by the footpath sign the 'Main Street' in Chelmorton is 1/2 mile away. The path follows the farm road all the way to the village, passing Shepley Farm on your left on the way. Chelmorton is the highest limestone village in Derbyshire at 1,200 feet. Turn left on reaching the Main Street, passing the Church Inn on your left. As you ascend out of the village the church, dedicated to St. John the Baptist, is on your right. Part of it dates back to Norman times; the weather vane on the top of the spire is unusual, being a grasshopper. At the top of the walled lane you turn right following a path between the walls which are almost field size apart. There are a lot of mounds left from lead mining times and in early summer the area is full of both yellow and blue mountain pansies. Keep to the right-hand wall and after 1/4 mile you reach a stile and walled lane. Cross over and follow the signposted path to Taddington, 1 1/2 miles away. When you get to Chelmorton the path sign says 2 miles!

From the lane the first field is open until you reach the stile, then as you gradually ascend towards the trig point 438 metres, you keep the stone wall on your left all the time, coming to all the stiles en route. After the third field you cross another walled lane. After passing the trig point in the field to your left you bear right slightly aiming for the right-hand side of a small reservoir. After this stile you begin descending as you head for Taddington, using the church spire as your guide. Cross a small road and a further field brings you into the village, via a path between the houses. Turn left and almost immediately keep straight ahead through a wrought iron gate and follow the path to Taddington church, which dates back to the 14th century. At the church turn left to the stile complete with wooden door and follow the path beside the wall on your right to the A6 dual carriageway road.

Cross the road to the stile on your right. Turn left after ascending it and follow the grass lane to the minor road to Priestcliffe. Turn right and walk down this road to the village 1/2 mile away. At the road junction in the village bear right then left soon afterwards and follow a walled grass lane, now heading northwards. After 1/3 mile along here, and where the lane turns sharp left, you keep straight ahead along the sign posted footpath and begin the descent to Miller's Dale. The stiles are there although the path at first is rather faint. At the end of the third field you begin descending steeply through a reserve of the Derbyshire Naturalists' Trust. The path is well defined and signed. It is very steep in places and on your right are the remains of a limestone quarry. Upon reaching the B6049 turn right and cross the River Wye before left and left again almost immediately to follow the path through Chee Dale.

The path hugs the right-hand side of the River Wye almost all the way. The abandoned Midland Railway line above is now the Monsal Trail, but I strongly advise following the path through the dale for it is quite an adventure! For the first 2/3 of a mile the path weaves its way close to the river and passes under a railway arch, before reaching a footbridge over the Wye. You keep to the right-hand side of the river; the bridge is a path from Blackwell to Wormhill. Barely 1/4 mile later the path bears right at Wormhill Springs which is renowned for its watercress. Cross the stream and ascend the wooden stile and continue up Chee Dale. You are now high above the river but you descend to it and gaze at the sheer 200 ft. walls of Chee Tor. The path hugs the river and goes under several overhangs before reaching a footbridge. Cross this and walk up the northern side a short distance before using another footbridge to return you to the right-hand side. The path now becomes interesting for in places you walk along stepping stones to get you up the dale.

For the rest of the dale to the Railway Cottages, you keep to the right-hand side. As you walk close to the river you can see opposite the highest limestone buttress in Derbyshire, about 270 feet high with a vicious overhang about 100 feet up it. It is a very popular rock climbing route. At the cottages you turn left and cross a long footbridge over the river. Now you walk up a rough track with the river on your right, passing underneath three railway bridges. About 1/3 mile from the footbridge you reach the car park and the A6 road. Topley Pike opposite is rich in limestone which here is about 2,700 feet thick, the thickest in Derbyshire.

HASSOP - 7 MILES

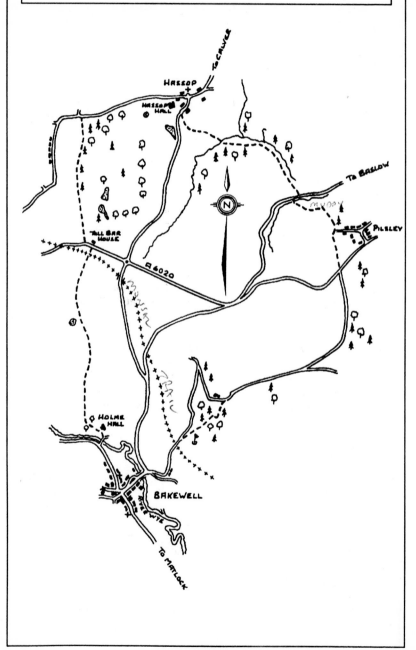

HASSOP - 7 MILES
- allow 2 1/2 hours

· · · *- Bakewell—Holme Hall—A6020—Long Rake Planta-tion—Hassop—Birchill Bank Wood— Pilsley—Paddocks Planta-tion—Ball Cross—Station Road—Bakewell.*

 - Several public car parks in central Bakewell.

 - 1:25,000 Outdoor Leisure Map—The White Peak - East sheet.

- numerous in Bakewell including - The Castle Inn, The Peacock, The Red Lion, The Queens Arms etc.; Eyre Arms Inn, Hassop. Devonshire Arms, Pilsley.

ABOUT THE WALK - Bakewell is the central hub of the Peak District and an admirable starting point for walks. On its doorstep are such renowned places as Lathkill Dale, Monsal Dale and Haddon Hall. This circular walk takes you through some very pleasant walking country and woodland passing at the half way point the village of Hassop. It is a small village but it does contain three interesting buildings and has a fascinating legend. As you return to Bakewell you have rewarding views of the town.

WALKING INSTRUCTIONS - The walk starts from the Rutland Arms Hotel in the centre of Bakewell, built in 1804 on the site of the White Horse Inn. It was in this hotel in 1859 that the cook made a mistake and created the first Bakewell Pudding. From the hotel follow the A6 road towards Buxton. After 1/4 mile near the 40 m.p.h. sign turn right and cross the packhorse bridge over the River Wye. Known as Holme Bridge, it was built in 1664. Keep straight ahead once across the bridge, and begin walking up the rough track on the immediate right-hand side of Holme Hall, a Tudor building erected in 1626. The track swings left before ascending steeply to a gate with a stile on the right. Continue climbing up a grass field along the line of a track to the field's northern end. Here is a gate and stile on the right. Keep straight ahead and for the next 3/4 mile you walk along a gated and walled lane. In the central section there is no wall on your left. After 3/4 mile cross the abandoned Bakewell-Buxton railway line - now the Monsal Trail and gain the A6020 road opposite Toll Bar House.

Turn left along the A6020 road for a few yards to the footpath sign on your right. The stile is on the left of the gate. Head almost due north across the field to the tall limestone boundary wall of Hassop Hall. The path line is not in evidence but soon after reaching the wall it becomes well defined. Keep the wall on your right and at every field boundary you will find a stile. Over the wall are the trees of Long Rake Plantation. Upon reaching the road, 1/2 mile from where you first reached the wall, turn right as signposted—Hassop 1/2 mile. As you near Hassop you descend the road with a row of yew trees on your left.

At the road junction in Hassop, the church is on your left and the hall on your right. The Catholic church, dedicated to All Saints, was built in 1816 and is an example of Classical Revival style. It is a gem of a building and very unusual for Derbyshire, it was built as a private chapel for the Eyre family . Just along the road to Calver is the Eyre Arms Inn. The Eyre family were great landowners and had more than twenty halls in Derbyshire, together with more than 20,000 acres of land. Hassop Hall was built by them in the early 17th century and has had an interesting past. During Henry Vll's reign the Eyres had to pay out £21,000 to get the hall back, having allowed it to be garrisoned by the losing side!

At the road junction turn right on the road signposted for Bakewell. After a few yards you pass a third architectural delight of Hassop, the 17th century Manor House on your right. Notice the post box set into the wall. Immediately past the farm on your left turn left up a walled lane and walk round the southern base of a small pronounced hillock. There are stiles on the right of the gates. About 1/4 mile from the road, at the eastern end of the small hill, bear right down a walled lane and cross a footbridge and enter Birchill Bank Wood. Just after the footbridge the path bears left to a well defined track. Turn left and follow this track through the trees and after 1/4 mile you reach open fields with the wood on your left. A 1/4 mile later is the main Baslow-Bakewell road, the A619.

Turn right and almost immediately left along another walled lane. This curves round to your left before gently ascending in a large curve to the western edge of Pilsley village. You can cut the corner off by following a right-of-way that heads straight up the field on your right and uses stone stiles. At the junction of the road into Pilsley keep straight ahead along a walled lane. In the final stages you ascend a stone stile with a hand rail and cross a field to the minor road, B6040 Pilsley to Bakewell.

Gaining the road you are opposite another minor road that leads over to Ball Cross Farm and Bakewell. It is along this road you now walk for the next mile. After a little over 1/2 mile of climbing past Paddocks Plantation the road levels off and a track from Edensor comes in from your left. Close to this junction on your left you can see an old stone road sign dated 1709; on one side you can read legibly—'Bakewell Rode. '

Continue along the road for about 1/3 mile to where it turns sharp right past Ball Cross Farm. Here you keep straight ahead and descend through the trees. Emerging from them you have an excellent view of Bakewell and its noble church. Cross the golf course by the well defined path and reach Station Road. Turn left and descend this road to the 13th century live arched bridge over the River Wye. Over this you are back in central Bakewell ready for a cup of tea and a Bakewell Pudding!

RIVER WYE BRIDGE, BAKEWELL
J.J.CREBER

THE DALES OF LATHKILL
- 7 MILES

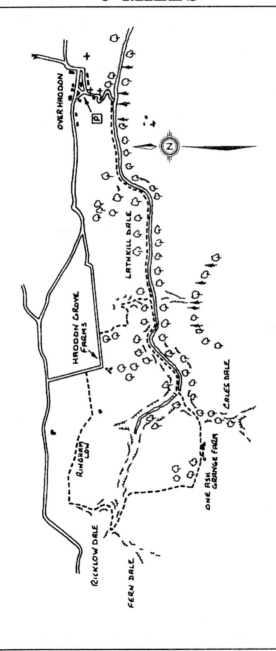

THE DALES OF LATHKILL - 7 MILES - allow 2 1/2 hours.

 - Over Haddon—Lathkill Dale—Haddon Grove Farm—Ricklow Dale—One Ash Grange Farm— Cales Dale— Lathkill Dale—Over Haddon.

- Over Haddon. Grid Ref. SK203664.

- 1:25,000 Outdoor Leisure Map—The White Peak - East sheet.

- Lathkill Hotel, Over Haddon.

ABOUT THE WALK - The beauty of Lathkill Dale is well known and a walk through the valley has few equals for attractive scenery. Off the dale are several smaller ones and on this walk we pass through three of these and see two others.

WALKING INSTRUCTIONS - From the car park in Over Haddon descend the 'No Through Road' as it zig-zags its way down to Lathkill Dale. Just before reaching the river turn right through the wooden stile and begin walking up the dale with the Lathkill river, the clearest in Britain, on your left. You walk up the broad track for the next mile and are now in part of the Derbyshire Dales National Nature Reserve. An abundance of flowers can be seen through the seasons and dippers are usually spotted. As you walk along you pass the ruins of lead mining with an engine house on your right and the pillars of an aqueduct on your left.

After a little over a mile you come to a fence and the end of the woodland. Keep straight ahead for a short distance before turning right up a wide grass track. You climb up a shallow dale and after 1/4 mile the track switches sharply to the left as you walk round a rock face to gain open country. Continue along the track passing a farm on your left to the minor road. Turn left and right at the entrance gates to Haddon Grove

Farm. At the field boundary of the first field on your left, go through the gate and walk along a track. Near the end of the second field and where the track turns left to a house, keep straight ahead to the stone stile. After this stile bear right to the next stile and follow the subsequent stiles through the field on the immediate north of Ringham Low, a burial chamber dating back to about 2,300 B.C. There were four chambers and one excavated in 1859 had the bones of twelve skeletons.

Four more fields from the Low, walking in a westerly direction, brings you to the floor of Ricklow Dale. Turn left and walk down the valley. Before you reach the old quarry and ruined buildings, turn right up a faint track and curve round the head of the dale and descend to a gate and stile and the entrance to Fern Dale. Ricklow Quarry was operative until the beginning of this century; here was mined Crinoidal limestone.

At the gate you are back in Lathkill Dale but instead of turning left and descending the dale, use the stile on the left of the gate and follow the farm track above the dale. After 1/4 mile the track heads south towards One Ash Grange Farm. Follow the track to the farm, turning left at the next gate. On approaching the farm, walk round its left-hand side as indicated by the footpath signs. Past the farm you are heading due east and approaching Cales Dale. The path through the dale, on its left-hand side, is walking at its best. You gradually descend to a footbridge over the Lathkill river. Across this you turn right for Over Haddon, 2 1/2 miles away.

You now walk with the river on your right as you wander down the dale, past waterfalls, weirs, high rocky sides, open stretches of water scarcely moving, and back into the woodland that you first walked through. On gaining the road at Lathkill Lodge, turn left and ascend the switchback road back to the car park. Thus ends a walk through part of the finest scenery in the Peak District.

THE HIKER'S CODE

❀ *Hike only along marked routes - do not leave the trail.*

❀ *Use stiles to climb fences; close gates.*

❀ *Camp only in designated campsites.*

❀ *Carry a light-weight stove.*

❀ *Leave the trail cleaner than you found it.*

❀ *Leave flowers and plants for others to enjoy.*

❀ *Keep dogs on a leash.*

❀ *Protect and do not disturb wildlife.*

❀ *Use the trail at your own risk.*

❀ *Leave only your thanks and footprints - take nothing but photographs.*

BRADFORD, GRATTON AND LONG DALE - 6 MILES

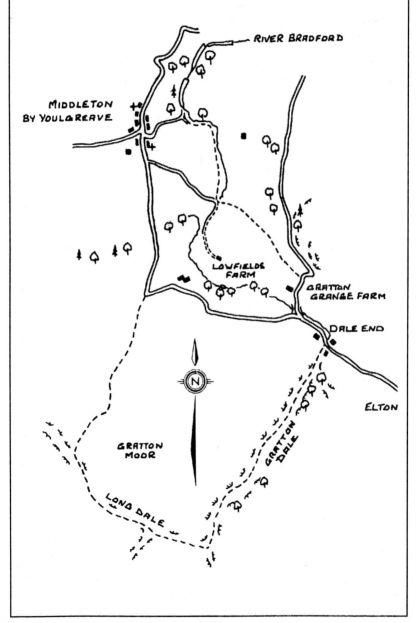

RIVER BRADFORD

MIDDLETON
BY YOULGREAVE

LOWFIELDS
FARM

GRATTON
GRANGE FARM

DALE END

ELTON

GRATTON
MOOR

GRATTON
DALE

LONG DALE

N

BRADFORD, GRATTON AND LONG DALE
- 6 MILES
- allow 2 1/2 hours.

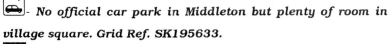

- Middleton-by-Youlgreave — Bradford Dale — Gratton Grange Farm — Dale End— Gratton Dale—Long Dale—Middleton-by-Youlgreave.

- No official car park in Middleton but plenty of room in village square. Grid Ref. SK195633.

- 1:25,000 Outdoor Leisure Map—The White Peak - East sheet.

- None on the walk! Nearest at Youlgreave or Elton.

ABOUT THE WALK - Begins from a very picturesque and unspoilt village—Middleton-by-Youlgreave—where many of the buildings date back to the early 19th century. The village is rich in history and has the tomb of Thomas Bateman (on private land) who died aged 39 in 1861. He lived nearby and is renowned for his local archaeological work, many of his finds now being in Weston Park Museum, Sheffield. A you re-enter the village you have splendid views of Middleton Hall from your walk, whilst as you came into the village of Youlgreave you will have seen on your left the ruins of Middleton Castle. This fortified mansion was the home of the Fulwood family. During the Civil War Sir Christopher Fulwood was an ardent Royalist but eventually he was cornered by the Parliamentarians and shot in Bradford Dale. You pass the rock where he was murdered. The walk is through pleasant and peaceful limestone country where on a summer's day you can lie back on the grass and listen to the skylarks above.

WALKING INSTRUCTIONS - Leave the village square by the east side down a lane opposite the Jubilee tree. Almost immediately you pass Tor Farm on your left. The lane soon becomes a rough walled track as it descends a shallow limestone gorge to the infant River Bradford 1/4 mile away. Just before the river, which is really a stream, turn right along a well defined footpath. A few yards along here you cross a stone slab bridge over a spring before crossing the 'River Bradford' via a concrete bridge with hand rail. Bear right and aim for the wooden steps. As you near them on your left is a large limestone boulder. It was here almost 350 years ago that Sir Christopher Fulwood was shot. At the top of the steps turn right past the pine trees and 100 yards later turn right across another stone slabbed bridge over the River Bradford. The path line across the next seven fields, as you head due south, is distinct and at all the walls are stone stiles.

Upon reaching the farm road to Lowfields Farm turn left just before the cattle grid to the wooden stile 20 yards away. The path from here to the road just above Gratton Grange Farm is not defined but the path line is simple to follow. First walk round the barbed wire enclosure on your right and gently ascend to another wooden stile. You now keep the electricity pylons on your left for much of the next field before crossing under them and keeping them on your right for 1/4 mile. You then keep them on your immediate left as you cross the brow of the field and head for a walled path to the road. The path here is clearly defined. Turn right at the road passing Gratton Grange Farm on your right. At the road junction beyond turn left to the cluster of houses at Dale End. On the right of the telephone kiosk in Dale End is the footpath sign and stile for entrance into Gratton Dale.

For much of the next mile through Gratton Dale you walk along a farm track. Cattle from Dale End Farm generally inhabit the first l/2 mile of the valley and in the winter time this section can be very muddy. However, beyond this the dale scenery is excellent with limestone outcrops and a small pine plantation on your right. At the end of the dale go through the wooden gate and turn right through a metal gate and begin walking through the shallow Long Dale. Walk along the valley floor for about 1/2 mile until you meet a stone wall crossing the dale . Here you bear right beside the wall before crossing over. Instead of keeping to the valley floor ascend the distinct grass track up the dale side. Upon reaching the stone wall on your right at the top, about 250 yards later, go through the gate on your right and follow the track with the stone wall on your right for two fields. Then it becomes a walled lane with gates. Keep to the track for the next half mile as it descends to the lane to the west of Smerrill Grange.

At the lane keep straight ahead for the final 3/4 mile back to Middleton-by-Youlgreave. As you walk along you have extensive views towards Bakewell. You finally descend gently into Middleton with Middleton Hall through the trees on your left. The hall dates from the early 19th century and is a splendid building. The village square is just ahead.

OBSTRUCTION OF RIGHT OF WAY

Description of Right of Way
(e,g, "Footpath from Dovedale to Ilam")

_____
_____
_____

Nature of Obstruction
(e.g. Locked gate, barbed wire across path etc.,)

_____
_____

Location of Obstruction
(Give Grid Reference if possible.)

_____
_____

Date of discovery of obstruction

_____

Name and address of person making report -

_____
_____
_____
_____

- you may photocopy this form -

Send to -

the local Rambler's Association
Footpath officer
or
The Footpath Inspector,
Derbyshire County Council

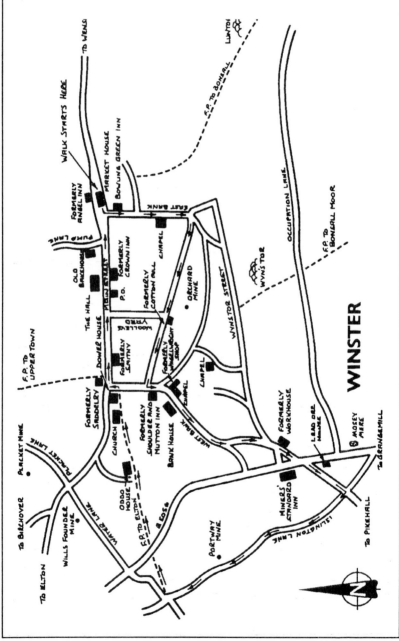

WINSTER - 2 MILES

WINSTER

38

WINSTER - 2 MILES
- allow 1 1/2 hours.

 - *Market House—West Bank—Miners' Standard Inn— Islington Lane - Market House.*

 - *No official car park in Winster.*

 - *1:25,000 Outdoor Leisure Map—The White Peak - East sheet.*

- *The Hall, The Bowling Green, The Miner's Standard in Winster.*

ABOUT THE WALK - Winster is my home village and a place for which I have a great respect. It was a very successful lead mining centre in the 18th century with more than 2,000 people and some, thirty inns ! Today the population is about 700 and there are only three inns! The village's prosperous past is reflected in its buildings and, despite its small size, more than eighty of these are 'listed'. This short circular walk takes you around Winster and the surrounding area and I hope gives you an insight into one of the limestone villages of the Peak District.

WALKING INSTRUCTIONS - The walk starts from the Market House—two storeys high and standing in the Main Street. The lower storey of thick gritstone blocks is 16th century, originally the five filled-in arches would have been open, in common with usual market house design. The upper storey is 18th century and probably replaces a timber construction. By the end of the last century the house was in a decaying state and the upper storey had to be removed. At the beginning of this century the building was given to the National Trust in 1906, becoming their first property in Derbyshire. The upper storey was then rebuilt, using the original material where possible, at a cost of £165. The building now serves as a National Trust Information

Centre and shop and is open to the public during the summer months on Saturday and Sunday afternoons—2 p.m. to 6 p.m.

From the Market House, turn left up East Bank, passing the Bowling Green Inn on your left and later a Wesleyan Chapel dated 1823 on your right. A little past the chapel turn right along a 'gennel' giving excellent views of the village as you walk past the top of Woolley's Yard to West Bank. As you do so you pass the mound of Orchard Mine on your left. Notice too the splendid architecture of the houses on East Bank and Woolley's Yard. At West Bank turn left and ascend the road past the former Shoulder of Mutton Inn and Wheelwright Shop, Bank House and the former Workhouse near the minor road (B5056) and close to the Miners' Standard Inn.

Wheelwright Shop: Now known as Yew Cottage. Believed to have been built in 1760. The earliest known deeds date from 1847 when the cottage and cowhouse were sold for £150 to George Henstock, a wheelwright. The house opposite built at the beginning of this century is on the site of another wheel wright shop.

Bank House: Built about 1580. A plaque on the right-hand side of the doorway records that the house has been the home of the village doctor for more than 100 years. The lawn outside the front door was the scene of a murder. On May 22nd, 1821, William Cuddie, the surgeon and apothecary of Winster, was murdered by William Brittlebank of Oddo. For a while there was a reward of £100 for the capture of Brittlebank who was 27 years old and 5 ft. 8 in. tall. Naturally, he had vanished. William Cuddie's tombstone can be seen in the churchyard and is on the right-hand side of the pair of trees, forming an arch over the path, when approached from West Bank.

Workhouse: The workhouse was established in 1744 and had nine rules for the management of the occupiers. The seventh rule was 'When any of the poor be employed out of the house the Overseer shall take the benefit of their work for their better maintenance and relief.' John Johnson was appointed in charge of the workhouse in 1744 for the salary of £10 per annum. Two entries from the overseers' accounts read: 'April 18th, 1752—I child's coffin, 2s. 6d. (12 1/2p) ; October 28th, 1765—£3 1Os. (£3.50p) for 28 weeks of milk .

Miner's Standard Inn: The name is almost the only reminder of the once prolific lead mining industry in the area. The inn was built in 1653 and over the doorway can be seen the date and the initials 'E.P.; E.P.; F.P.' They stand for Edith, Ella and Frank Price, although they were often said to mean - *"Every person entering pays for a pint!"*

Cross the road - B5056 - to the left of the inn and walk along the road signposted for Newhaven.

Lead Ore House & Mosey Mere - Just to your left can be seen a
Lead Ore House, used by lead miner's as an overnight safe, 50 years
ago. Just beyond is Mosey Mere - the water was used by the villagers
of Islington. The water lies on volcanic rock and cannot seep through
the limestone underneath.

After approximately 75 yards, turn right down a walled lane, known
as Islington Lane . As you walk down you pass close to the site of
Islington village on your left and Portway Mine on your right. After a
mile at the junction of a farm road on your left, turn right, as footpath
signposted, and walk across the fields past Oddo House and into the
churchyard. As you do so look to your left. You are in limestone country
but scarcely a mile away is the gritstone country and the outcrops of
Cratcliffe and Robin Hood's Stride.

Oddo House: This is the third house to occupy this site. Oddo is
associated with the Brittlebank family who first came to Winster in
1700 when Hugh Brittlebank an assistant solicitor and his wife moved
here. A later Brittlebank became renowned for the murder he commit-
ted in 1821 on the lawn of Bank House. The Brittlebank's left Oddo in
1891 when their house was described as a 'modern residence erected
in substantial manner, regardless of cost.' They also owned a consid-
erable amount of the village and together with the house were sold
three farms, 68 'lots choice accommodation' and 'meadow and pasture
land'. The total area was 273 acres, 2 roods and 4 perches. The walk
through Oddo to the church is particularly attractive and grey squir-
rels are frequently seen in the trees close to the churchyard.

Church: Dedicated to St. John the Baptist. Winster was formerly one
of five chapelries connected to Youlgreave. In 1650 the Parliamentary
Commissioner suggested that Elton and Winster be united into one
parish. Today both are individual parishes but the living combines
both, with the vicar living at Winster. The church, apart from the tower
which was built in 1721, was rebuilt and enlarged in 1842 for the cost
of about £1,600. In 1883 it was enlarged again into the building we see
today. The interior has two aisles with three quatrefoil shafts in the
middle; they are surprisingly thin but in keeping. The one nearest the
chancel joins the chancel arch by means of two arches. The font has
always been regarded with curiosity and its date is uncertain; Pevsner
states that it could be a Tudor imitation of Norman workmanship. The
clock was fitted in 1846 and cost £80.

From the church accounts, which make interesting reading, we learn
that the five bells were brought to the church for a cost of £20 16s. 9d.
(£20.84p) and were hung by Jacob Holmes for £3 8s. 0d. (£3.40p) The

bell ropes cost seven shillings (35p). During the 18th century there was a permanent mole catcher and in 1737 he received £3 a year for the service. Whilst many children died very young—four months, eight months and thirteen months old, for instance—many people lived to great ages. One woman, Ann Hawley, died on 8th March, 1661, 'above 100 years old'. The oldest man was John Rains, buried on December 13th, 1 88 1, aged 97 years. Another member of the Rains family was Joseph Rains who was buried on November 4th, 1866, aged 62. A notice at the rear of the Burial Register records the event

'Found dead in River Derwent, November 3rd. Verdict—accidental death. He was a well known character in the village—thoroughly clean and honest—for many years was a servant of the late Andrew Brittlebank Esq., and was often entrusted by him with large sums of money, all of which, though he was frequently intoxicated, he brought safely (he is known to have hidden it in his shoe and to have walked from the Bank in Wirksworth with it in that position).

'On Sunday, October 21st, he went to Matlock and was never seen alive again—and though every means was used and no expense spared to recover the body all efforts failed—until November 3rd. The body was seen floating quietly down the stream of the River Derwent at Matlock. He is supposed to have attempted to return to Winster at night by the foot road along the meadows from Matlock Bridge (where he was last seen), to have missed his footing and fallen into the river.'

A further entry refers to Catherine Orme, buried February 10th, 1866, aged 39: *'Found dead—February 7th—having hung herself from the house beam. Verdict of the jury—Temporary insanity.'*

Another in 1874 refers to Kathleen Mary Higgins, buried January 21st, aged 16 months: *"died from sucking 'lucifer matches".*

There are many entries to deaths down the lead mines and of persons falling down shafts, such as *"Anthony Hardy, came to his death by falling down a shaft at a mine called Mill Close within the liberty of Wensley in the Parish of Darley, l9th July 1823, aged 15 years."* *"Joseph Beardow was buried on September 18th, 1870, aged 46 after being 'crushed to death by a wheel (water wheel) at Ecclestor Mine at 4 o'clock in the afternoon of Thursday, September 15.'*

From the churchyard walk past the walls of the Dower House and on to West Bank. Turn left before turning right and walking along the Main Street back to the Market House. As you do so you see the Dower House, the 18th century three storey high buildings of the Main Street, the Hall and the old Bakehouse at the start of Pump Lane. Only in the last decade has the bakery ceased operating.

Dower House: Dates from the 16th century. Has been much altered as can be seen today by the various blocked windows. It was first altered in 1600. Notice the carved front gates and how the main street turns abruptly right to squeeze past the house. Originally this was a right-of-way from Oddo to the village and was made into a road last century thereby slicing into the grounds of the house.

The Hall: Erected in 1628 by Francis Moore. The gritstone, with which the hall is built was brought from Winster on pack horses from Stancliffe Quarries in Darley Dale. The ceilings in the lower rooms had frescoes by West, the successor of Sir Joshua Reynolds as President of the Royal Academy. Later the hall was occupied by a member of the clergy who objected to the semi-nude nymphs and had them white-washed over. Today the building has been converted to an inn.

A few steps from the hall brings you back to the Market House.

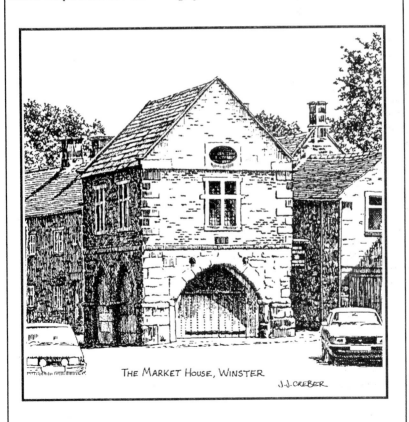

THE MARKET HOUSE, WINSTER

J.J. CREBER

PARWICH - 6 MILES

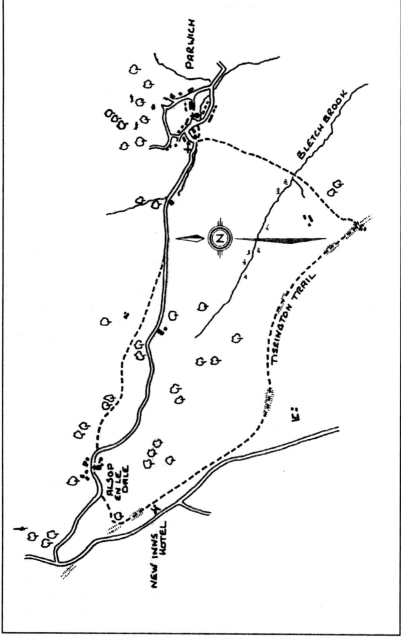

PARWICH - 6 MILES
- allow 2 1/2 hours.

⬛ ⬛ ⬛ - *Parwich—Bletch Brook—Tissington Trail— Alsop-en-le-Dale—Parwich.*

- *No official car park in Parwich.*

 - *O.S. 1:25,000 Outdoor Leisure Map—The White Peak - East Sheet.*

 - *Sycamore Inn, Parwich. New Inns Hotel near Tissington Trail.*

ABOUT THE WALK - Parwich is a delightful limestone village off the beaten track and full of interest. The church was largely rebuilt in 1872 but does contain a Norman tympanum. On the northern side is Parwich Hall, built in the mid 18th century and unusual for the Peak District in being largely constructed from red brick. As you climb out of the village you have splendid views of this building and over the village.

WALKING INSTRUCTIONS - Begin the walk from the green in the centre of the village and walk up the road away from the church. After a short distance turn left and follow the road signposted to Alsop-en-le-Dale. As you walk along here, between the houses, you pass the Parwich British Legion Club on your right. Soon afterwards the road turns sharp right and on the left-hand side can be seen the stile and path sign to Tissington, two miles away.

Turn left and follow this path, first crossing the field to a stile from where the best views of Parwich village are seen. Then you ascend more steeply to the top of the ridge. As you gently drop down the other side your fourth stile from the road is behind a holly bush. Through this stile you descend sharply to the footbridge over Bletch Brook. Across this you begin climbing once more to the farm track to Shaw's Farm on your right, three fields away. A wooden stile brings you to the track and the footpath sign here tells you you have walked 1 1/2 miles. Bear left and cross the bridge over the Tissington Trail. On its left-hand side is the path down to the Trail; take this and turn left and begin walking up the wide track. If you have time and energy to spare, you can walk into Tissington village to see the hall, church and village pond before gaining the Trail there. This will add about 1 1/2 miles on to your walk.

As you walk along the Trail you have distant views of the surrounding area. sometimes you are in a cutting, other times you are on a platform enjoying a 360 degree view. Little over a mile from where you joined the Trail you near the A515 Buxton-Ashbourne road. About 3/4 mile later you pass the New Inns Hotel on your left which has an access path from the Trail—at just over half way a refreshment might not seem a bad idea. Beyond the inn you reach Alsop-en-le-Dale car park and picnic site. At the other side of the car park, indicated by a footpath sign, leave the Trail and cross a stile and begin descending to Alsop village. You walk close to a wall on your right to a stile. Through this you keep the wall on your left to the road in the bottom.

Turn right at the road and into Alsop-en-le-Dale. It is a delightful spot, totally unspoilt, with farms, hall and small church. The church is dedicated to St. Michael and All Angels and has a Norman doorway, the tower was built in 1883. Opposite the church is a twin gabled hall built in the 17th century. Continue through the village to its southern side. On your left is Manor Cottage and at the end of the garden, on the right of it, is the stone stepped stile and path to Parwich. You diagonally climb the first field on your right to another stone stepped stile and continue ascending through the next field to a further stone stile. Here the path levels off as you keep to the left of a dew pond to reach a stile and path just inside a small wood. Walk through the wood keeping close to its right-hand side to another stile. Cross the field beyond to a further stile. From here you are descending all the way back to Parwich. The next stile is not there so you have to use the gate. Through this you can see the next two stiles as you cross the fields on the right of Peakway. In the next field you cannot see the stile at first but after a short distance it appears. Beyond it cross the road to Peakway and descend to the road using a stile over a small stream and reaching the road at the entrance to Middle hills Farm. Turn left and walk along the road to Parwich 1/3 mile away. You soon reach the place where you began the walk to the Tissington Trail and, instead of turning left through the village, keep straight ahead through a stile and follow the path beside the brook back to the green. When you reach the road the village green is on your left and Sycamore Inn is on your right.

WALK RECORD CHART

Date walked -

EYAM MOOR & WARDLOW - 12 MILES ....

BASLOW EDGE & CHATSWORTH PARK - 6 MILES ....

MONSAL DALE - HIGH LEVEL ROUTE - 7 MILES ....

MONSAL DALE - LOW LEVEL ROUTE - 1 1/2 MILES ....

CHEE DALE & CHELMORTON - 9 MILES ....

HASSOP - 7 MILES ....

THE DALES OF LATHKILL - 7 MILES ....

BRADFORD, GRATTON & LONG DALE - 6 MILES ....

WINSTER - 2 MILES ....

PARWICH - 6 MILES ....

JOHN MERRILL'S WALKING BADGE

GET A JOHN MERRILL LONG WALK BADGE - Complete six
of these walks and send a copy of the Walk Record Chart and £2.50
to J.N.M. Publications for a signed certificate and badge - 3 1/2
diameter and four colour embroidered on a blue cloth.

BADGE ORDER FORM

Dates completed ....

....

Name

....

Address

....

....

"I've done a John Merrill Walk" T shirt - Emerald Green with
white lettering - all sizes - £7.00 including postage and VAT.

From - J.N.M. Publications, Winster, Matlock,
Derbyshire. DE4 2DQ

TEL. Winster - 0629 - 650454 (24 hrs.)
Fax: Winster - 0629 - 650416

.... You may photocopy this form if needed ....

48